WORKBOOK

Cambridge IGCSE™ and O Level

Economics

Third Edition

Paul Hoang

hachette
LEARNING

Introduction

Welcome to the Cambridge IGCSE™ and O Level Economics Workbook. The aim of this Workbook is to provide you with further opportunity to practise the skills you have acquired through using the Cambridge IGCSE™ and O Level Economics Student's Book. It is designed to complement the third edition of the Student's Book (ISBN 978 1036 010 737) and to provide additional exercises to help you in your preparation for your examinations.

The chapters in this Workbook reflect the topics in the Student's Book. There is no set way to approach using this Workbook. You may wish to use it to supplement your understanding of the different topics as you work through each chapter of the textbook, or you may prefer to use it to reinforce your skills in dealing with particular topics as you prepare for examination. The Workbook is intended to be sufficiently flexible to suit whatever you feel is the best approach for your needs. Answer lines have been provided but do not necessarily indicate length of response. You may need additional paper for some questions, particularly those with a higher mark allocation.

This text has not been through the endorsement process for the Cambridge Pathway. Any references or materials related to answers, grades, papers or examinations are based on the opinion of the author.

The Cambridge International Education syllabus or curriculum framework associated assessment guidance material and specimen papers should always be referred to for definitive guidance.

The questions and sample answers that appear in this book were written by the author. In examinations, the way marks are awarded may be different.

Although every effort has been made to ensure that website addresses are correct at time of going to press, Hachette Learning cannot be held responsible for the content of any website mentioned in this book. It is sometimes possible to find a relocated web page by typing in the address of the home page for a website in the URL window of your browser.

Hachette UK's policy is to use papers that are natural, renewable and recyclable products and made from wood grown in well-managed forests and other controlled sources. The logging and manufacturing processes are expected to conform to the environmental regulations of the country of origin.

To order, please visit www.HachetteLearning.com or contact Customer Service at education@hachette.co.uk / +44 (0)1235 827827.

ISBN 9781036010751

© Paul Hoang 2025

First published in 2015
Second edition published in 2018
This edition published in 2025 by Hachette Learning
An Hachette UK Company
Carmelite House, 50 Victoria Embankment, London EC4Y 0DZ
www.HachetteLearning.com

The authorised representative in the EEA is Hachette Ireland, 8 Castlecourt Centre, Dublin 15, D15 XTP3, Ireland (email: info@hbgi.ie)

Impression number   10 9 8 7 6 5 4 3 2 1

Year   2029 2028 2027 2026 2025

All rights reserved. Apart from any use permitted under UK copyright law, no part of this publication may be reproduced or transmitted in any form or by any means, electronic or mechanical, including photocopying and recording, or held within any information storage and retrieval system, without permission in writing from the publisher or under licence from the Copyright Licensing Agency Limited. Further details of such licences (for reprographic reproduction) may be obtained from the Copyright Licensing Agency Limited, www.cla.co.uk.

Cover photo © Rawpixel.com – stock.adobe.com
Typeset in 11.5/13 ITC OfficinaSanStd-Book by Aptara, Inc.
Printed in the UK by Bell & Bain Limited

A catalogue record for this title is available from the British Library

Contents

SECTION 1 The basic economic problem
1 The nature of the basic economic problem — 4
2 The factors of production — 6
3 Opportunity cost — 8
4 Production possibility curve diagrams — 10

SECTION 2 The allocation of resources
5 The role of markets in allocating resources — 13
6 Demand — 15
7 Supply — 18
8 Price determination — 21
9 Price changes — 24
10 Price elasticity of demand — 26
11 Price elasticity of supply — 29
12 Market economic system — 32
13 Market failure — 34
14 Mixed economic system — 37

SECTION 3 Microeconomic decision-makers
15 Money and banking — 39
16 Households — 41
17 Workers — 43
18 Firms — 47
19 Firms and production — 49
20 Firms' costs, revenue and objectives — 51
21 Types of markets — 55

SECTION 4 Government and the macroeconomy
22 Government macroeconomic intervention — 58
23 Fiscal policy — 60
24 Monetary policy — 63
25 Supply-side policy — 65
26 Economic growth — 67
27 Employment and unemployment — 69
28 Inflation — 71

SECTION 5 Economic development
29 Living standards — 74
30 Poverty — 77
31 Population — 80
32 Differences in economic development between countries — 83

SECTION 6 International trade and globalisation
33 Specialisation and free trade — 86
34 Globalisation and trade restrictions — 88
35 Foreign exchange rates — 91
36 Current account of the balance of payments — 93

1 The basic economic problem

Student's Book Chapters 1–4

1 The nature of the basic economic problem

1 The basic economic problem is [1 mark]

  A how best to allocate scarce resources to satisfy unlimited needs and wants

  B how to satisfy limited wants and needs with unlimited resources

  C meeting increased demand for goods and services with limited resources

  D the interaction of market forces to satisfy unlimited needs and wants

2 An example of a free good is [1 mark]

  A housing

  B information in the public domain

  C running shoes

  D tennis rackets

3 Which of the following best describes the impact of scarcity on economic decision-making? [1 mark]

  A It eliminates the need for trade-offs in decision-making.

  B It forces governments to print more money to tackle economic problems.

  C It only affects low-income countries.

  D It requires economies to decide what, how and for whom to produce.

4 Which of the following is **not** one of the three basic economic questions addressed by an economy? [1 mark]

  A For whom should production take place?

  B How should production take place?

  C What production should take place?

  D When should production take place?

5 Which of the following is an example of a need? [1 mark]

  A new clothes

  C shelter (warmth)

  B an overseas holiday

  D a smartphone

1 The nature of the basic economic problem

6 Define 'public sector'. [2 marks]

....

....

7 Explain, using relevant examples, the difference between **needs** and **wants**. [4 marks]

....

....

....

....

8 Explain, using relevant examples, the difference between **economic goods** and **free goods**. [4 marks]

....

....

....

....

9 Explain, using examples, how **goods** differ from **services**. [4 marks]

....

....

....

....

10 Explain how poverty in the real world is an example of the basic economic problem. [4 marks]

....

....

....

....

1 THE BASIC ECONOMIC PROBLEM

2 The factors of production

1 Production of any good or service requires resources known as *[1 mark]*

  A factors of production
  B land
  C production facilities
  D raw materials

2 What is the generic name for the natural resources required in the production process? *[1 mark]*

  A capital
  B enterprise
  C labour
  D land

3 What is the name of the reward for use of enterprise in the production process? *[1 mark]*

  A income
  B profit
  C rent
  D salaries and wages

4 Which of the following best describes labour as a factor of production? *[1 mark]*

  A the business skills required to manage production
  B the human effort used in production
  C the manufactured tools and machinery used in production
  D the natural resources used in production

5 What is the name given to manufactured resources required in the production process? *[1 mark]*

  A capital
  B enterprise
  C labour
  D land

6 Describe, with the use of a relevant example, the meaning of **enterprise** as a factor of production. *[2 marks]*

....

....

7 Explain **two** causes of changes in the quantity and quality of factors of production. [4 marks]

....

....

....

....

8 Explain why labour, as a factor of production, is essential in the production process. [4 marks]

....

....

....

....

9 Explain, using at least **two** examples, how new technologies might affect the quantity and quality of factors of production in an economy. [4 marks]

....

....

....

....

10 Analyse, using relevant examples, how all **four** factors of production are needed in the production of a good or service of your choice. [6 marks]

....

....

....

....

....

1 THE BASIC ECONOMIC PROBLEM

3 Opportunity cost

1 Why does almost every economic choice made have an opportunity cost? *[1 mark]*

   A In most cases, there is an alternative option.

   B In most cases, there is no alternative option.

   C People have infinite wants.

   D Resources are not allocated efficiently.

2 Which of the following is **least** likely to be an opportunity cost of studying economics at university? *[1 mark]*

   A other things the money could be spent on instead of going to university

   B the difference in earning potential by attending university

   C the option to study geography at university

   D the option to work

3 From the data below, what is the opportunity cost of producing 1 kilogram (kg) of potatoes in terms of kilograms of carrots? *[1 mark]*

Carrots (kg)		Potatoes (kg)
65	plus	25
55	plus	30

   A 1 kg

   B 2 kg

   C 5 kg

   D 10 kg

4 From the table below, what is the opportunity cost of producing 1 extra unit of producer goods? *[1 mark]*

Producer goods (units)	Consumer goods (units)
30	52
33	43
36	34
39	25

   A 1 unit

   B 3 units

   C 6 units

   D 9 units

5 Yann bought a new bicycle for $350 but has never used it. The second-hand value of the bicycle is $250. What is the opportunity cost to Yann of keeping the bicycle? *[1 mark]*

   A $0

   B $100

   C $250

   D $350

3 Opportunity cost

6 Define 'opportunity cost'. *[2 marks]*

....

....

7 Explain the opportunity cost to society of the government using public funds to construct a new airport. *[4 marks]*

....

....

....

....

8 Colleen earns $10.50 an hour, but has chosen to take two hours off work in order to attend a school trip with her son to a theatre show. Her ticket costs $15. Calculate the opportunity cost of Colleen attending this school trip. *[2 marks]*

....

....

9 Sangita pays $30 for each one-hour driving lesson per week, taken over a 20-week period. In that time, she could have earned $18 per hour as a teaching assistant, or $12 per hour working in a local restaurant. Explain the opportunity cost to Sangita of her taking each driving lesson. *[2 marks]*

....

....

10 Tiga is an outstanding 14-year-old football player who has been spotted by a top London football club. They have offered him the opportunity to play full-time, on a scholarship of £35,000 ($45,900) per year for the next four years, with the intention of becoming professional within this time. Analyse the possible opportunity costs to Tiga if he decides to take up this offer. *[6 marks]*

....

....

....

....

....

1 THE BASIC ECONOMIC PROBLEM

4 Production possibility curve diagrams

1 Which of the following does **not** shift the production possibility curve (PPC) outwards? *[1 mark]*

　A higher prices 　　　　　　　　　　　**C** improved education and healthcare

　B higher productivity levels 　　　　　**D** technological advances

2 What do most economies strive to increase? *[1 mark]*

　A consumer goods 　　　　　　　　　　**C** productive capacity

　B opportunity cost 　　　　　　　　　　**D** unemployment

3 Which of the following is **most** likely to cause an outwards shift of an economy's PPC? *[1 mark]*

　A a fall in the quality of factors of production

　B a fall in the quantity of factors of production

　C an increase in the quantity of factors of production

　D higher levels of unemployment

Study the PPC diagram for Country X, which produces only two goods: wheat and oil. Use this diagram to answer Questions 4 to 6.

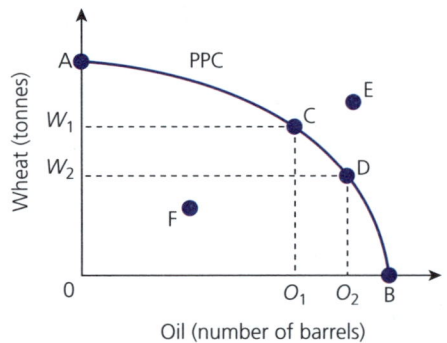

4 If Country X wishes to increase the production of wheat from W_2 to W_1, the opportunity cost in terms of oil is *[1 mark]*

　A a decrease in oil production from O_2 to O_1 　　**C** an outward shift of the PPC curve to point E

　B an increase in oil production from O_1 to O_2 　　**D** C to D

5 At which point on the PPC diagram of Country X is there spare capacity in the economy? *[1 mark]*

　A C 　　　　　　　　　　　　　　　　　**C** E

　B D 　　　　　　　　　　　　　　　　　**D** F

6 Describe **two** ways in which Country X could increase the productive capacity of the economy and cause its PPC curve to shift outwards to point E. [4 marks]

....

....

....

....

7 Define 'productive capacity'. [2 marks]

....

....

8 a Describe what a PPC diagram shows. [2 marks]

....

....

b Explain how the concept of opportunity cost is shown on a PPC diagram. [4 marks]

....

....

....

....

9 Explain the **two** conditions that must hold for an economy to be operating on its PPC. [4 marks]

....

....

....

....

1 THE BASIC ECONOMIC PROBLEM

10 Discuss, with the use of an appropriate diagram, the consequences of an outwards shift of the PPC for an economy. *[8 marks]*

2 The allocation of resources

Student's Book Chapters 5–14

5 The role of markets in allocating resources

1 Which of the following is **not** a key economic question addressed by all economies? [1 mark]

   A For whom should production take place?

   B How should production take place?

   C What production should take place?

   D Why should production take place?

2 What does **market equilibrium** refer to? [1 mark]

   A the point where both demand and supply decrease

   B the point where demand equals supply

   C the point where demand exceeds supply

   D the point where supply exceeds demand

3 What tends to happen in a market when the price of a product is below the market equilibrium price? [1 mark]

   A The market will clear immediately.

   B The product will be seen as too cheap.

   C The product will be seen as too expensive.

   D The supply of the product will exceed demand.

4 Which of the following is **not** a feature of the price mechanism? [1 mark]

   A Competition creates choice and opportunities for consumers.

   B Goods and services are allocated on the basis of price.

   C Government interference helps to correct market failures.

   D Resources are owned by private economic agents.

2 THE ALLOCATION OF RESOURCES

5 What role do buyers play in a market system? *[1 mark]*

    A They create demand for goods and services.

    B They create supply for goods and services.

    C They regulate market prices.

    D They set the prices for goods and services.

6 Define 'market'. *[2 marks]*

....

....

7 Explain **one** factor that can cause market disequilibrium to occur. *[2 marks]*

....

....

8 Explain the role of buyers and sellers in a market. *[4 marks]*

....

....

....

....

9 Explain, using examples, any **two** of the key questions about resource allocation in a market system. *[4 marks]*

....

....

....

....

10 Explain **two** reasons for a possible decline in the market supply of avocados. *[4 marks]*

....

....

....

....

6 Demand

1 The willingness and ability of customers to pay a given price to buy a good or service is known as [1 mark]

   A effective demand

   B market demand

   C quantity demanded

   D the law of demand

2 Which statement explains why there might be a decrease in the demand for sugar? [1 mark]

   A Consumers are more aware of the health issues related to sugar.

   B Demand for coffee and tea has increased.

   C New technologies increase the output of sugar.

   D There is an increase in the supply of land to produce sugar.

3 Which factor does **not** explain why the demand for cars in China has continuously increased? [1 mark]

   A effective advertising and marketing from car makers

   B greater household disposable incomes

   C higher interest rates in China

   D lower import taxes on cars made outside of China

4 Which products are considered to be complements? [1 mark]

   A apples and oranges

   B shampoo and conditioner

   C sugar and tea

   D tea and coffee

5 Which of the following is **not** a determinant of demand? [1 mark]

   A income   C subsidies

   B price   D substitutes

6 Explain why an ordinary demand curve is downward sloping. [2 marks]

   ....

   ....

2 THE ALLOCATION OF RESOURCES

7 Explain, using appropriate diagrams, the difference between a **movement along** the demand curve and a **shift** in demand. *[4 marks]*

....

....

....

....

8 Explain **two** factors that might affect the demand for ice cream. *[4 marks]*

....

....

....

....

9 Describe, using a relevant example, the difference between **individual demand** and **market demand** for a product. *[4 marks]*

....

....

....

....

6 Demand

10 Analyse, using an appropriate demand diagram, the impact on the demand for Coca-Cola following a successful advertising campaign by Pepsi. *[6 marks]*

....

....

....

....

....

....

2 THE ALLOCATION OF RESOURCES

7 Supply

1 The willingness and ability of firms to supply goods and services at a given price is known as *[1 mark]*

   A demand
   B equilibrium
   C supply
   D the law of supply

2 Which statement suggests why there might be a fall in the market supply of coal? *[1 mark]*

   A Consumer incomes have fallen.
   B New green technologies mean customers have switched to alternative energy sources.
   C The price of coal has increased.
   D There is a discovery of new coal supplies.

3 Which factor does **not** shift the supply curve of motor cars to the right? *[1 mark]*

   A an increase in household disposable incomes
   B high volume of stocks (inventories) of motor cars
   C improved technologies that enable motor cars to be produced at a faster rate
   D lower costs of production from moving production facilities to where labour is more affordable

4 Which of the following will cause a contraction in the supply of tomato sauce? *[1 mark]*

   A a fall in the price of tomato sauce
   B an increase in sales taxes of food products
   C a poor harvest of tomatoes
   D fewer farmers growing tomatoes

5 Which of the following is **not** a determinant of supply? *[1 mark]*

   A income
   B price
   C productive capacity
   D time

6 Explain why an ordinary supply curve is upward sloping. *[2 marks]*

   ....

   ....

7 Supply

7 Explain the difference between a **movement along** the supply curve and a **shift** in supply. *[4 marks]*

....

....

....

....

8 Explain **two** factors that might shift the supply curve of motor vehicles. *[4 marks]*

....

....

....

....

9 Explain, using an appropriate diagram, the impact on the supply of textbooks due to changes in the market price. *[4 marks]*

....

....

....

....

2 THE ALLOCATION OF RESOURCES

10 Analyse, using an appropriate diagram, how the imposition of a tax on suppliers of oil (petrol) affects the quantity supplied. *[6 marks]*

8 Price determination

Questions 1 to 3 refer to the following demand-and-supply schedule for smartphones:

Price per smartphone ($)	Quantity demanded ('000 units)	Quantity supplied ('000 units)
1,000	100	600
900	200	550
800	300	500
700	400	400
600	500	300
500	600	200
400	700	100

1 At what price does the market reach equilibrium? *[1 mark]*

   A $900

   B $800

   C $700

   D $600

2 What would happen if the price of smartphones was set at $1,000? *[1 mark]*

   A There would be an increase in market supply.

   B There would be excess demand.

   C There would be excess supply.

   D There would be market equilibrium.

3 What would happen in the market if the price of smartphones fell to $500? *[1 mark]*

   A The market would reach equilibrium.

   B The quantity demanded would be less than the quantity supplied.

   C There would be a shortage of smartphones.

   D There would be a surplus of smartphones.

4 Which situation exists when the price of a product is set above the market equilibrium price, thus creating a surplus in the market? *[1 mark]*

   A excess demand

   B excess supply

   C market disequilibrium

   D market equilibrium

2 THE ALLOCATION OF RESOURCES

5 The data below shows the demand-and-supply schedule for mushrooms each week. Which of the following statements is incorrect? *[1 mark]*

Supply	Price per unit ($)	Demand
21,000	10	18,000
20,000	9	20,000
19,000	8	22,000

A At $8 per unit, there is an excess demand of 3,000 units.

B At $10 per unit, there is an excess supply of 3,000 units.

C Equilibrium exists at $9 per unit.

D There is a shortage in the market at $10 per unit.

6 a Define 'market equilibrium'. *[2 marks]*

....

....

b Explain, using appropriate examples, the difference between a **shortage** and a **surplus**. *[4 marks]*

....

....

....

....

7 Explain **two** features of the price mechanism. *[4 marks]*

....

....

....

....

8 Explain the difference between **equilibrium price** and **disequilibrium price**. *[4 marks]*

....

....

....

....

8 Price determination

9 Explain, using a diagram, what is meant by **excess demand**. *[4 marks]*

....

....

....

....

10 Analyse, using an appropriate diagram, how the imposition of a subsidy on rice affects the market equilibrium price and quantity traded. *[6 marks]*

....

....

....

....

....

....

2 THE ALLOCATION OF RESOURCES

9 Price changes

1 Which of the following is the **most** probable outcome if a government raises the tax on the sale of tobacco products, as shown in the diagram below? *[1 mark]*

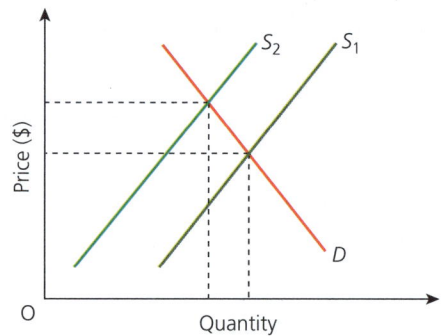

- **A** higher price and higher quantity traded
- **B** higher price and lower quantity traded
- **C** lower price and higher quantity traded
- **D** lower price and lower quantity traded

2 Which factor would **not** cause a rightward shift of the supply curve for the agricultural sector? *[1 mark]*

- **A** favourable weather conditions
- **B** government subsidies for farmers
- **C** higher costs of fertilisers (nutrients for plants)
- **D** technological progress in the agricultural sector

3 Which of the following factors would **not** cause a rightward shift of the demand curve for petrol cars? *[1 mark]*

- **A** effective persuasive advertising
- **B** higher disposable household income
- **C** significantly higher prices of electric cars
- **D** the imposition of a new vehicle registration tax

4 What is the general outcome if there is excess demand in a market? *[1 mark]*

- **A** The market price falls.
- **B** The market price falls but demand rises.
- **C** The market price rises.
- **D** The quantity traded rises.

5 What is **most** likely to occur in the market for Nike sports shoes following a fall in price of Adidas sports shoes? *[1 mark]*

- **A** The price falls and quantity demanded rises.
- **B** The price rises and quantity demanded falls.
- **C** The quantity demanded falls.
- **D** The quantity demanded rises.

9 Price changes

6 State **two** consequences of an increase in the number of wheat suppliers in the market. *[2 marks]*

....

....

7 Give **one** reason why technological progress might increase prices, and **one** reason why it might cause prices to fall. *[2 marks]*

....

....

8 Explain **two** consequences of government subsidies for manufacturers of electric vehicles. *[4 marks]*

....

....

....

....

9 Explain the impact of the imposition of higher fuel taxes on the market for motor vehicles. *[4 marks]*

....

....

....

....

10 Starbucks opened its first store in China in 1999 in Beijing. In 2017, the coffee retailer opened its largest outlet: a store of almost 2,800 square metres in Shanghai, China, capable of serving up to 550 customers at one time. By 2023, Starbucks had over 6,000 stores across China, making it one of the largest markets for the company outside the United States. The company aims to have 9,000 stores in China by 2025. Explain **two** factors that may have increased the demand for Starbucks coffee in China. *[4 marks]*

....

....

....

....

2 THE ALLOCATION OF RESOURCES

10 Price elasticity of demand

1 What is the value of price elasticity of demand (PED) for a product for which a 10% price rise reduces the quantity demanded by 8%? *[1 mark]*

　A −1.25

　B −0.8

　C +0.8

　D +1.25

2 Based on the following information, what is the value of PED for potatoes? *[1 mark]*

Change in price	Change in demand
+5%	−1%

　A −5.0

　B −0.2

　C +0.2

　D +5.0

3 What do economists calculate using PED? *[1 mark]*

　A changes in the average price level in the economy

　B changes in the production costs of firms due to price changes

　C how sensitive consumers are to price changes

　D the market price that generates the largest amount of profit for firms

4 With reference to the diagram below, what will happen to the firm's total revenue? *[1 mark]*

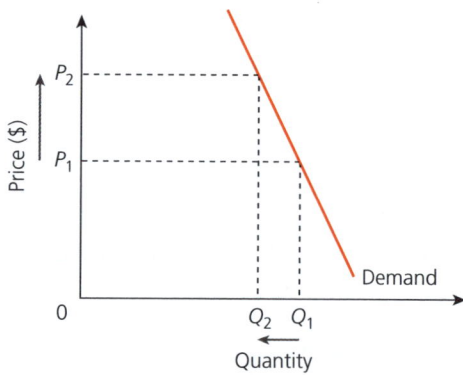

　A Total revenue will decrease.

　B Total revenue will fall from $P_1 \times Q_1$ to $P_2 \times Q_2$.

　C Total revenue will increase.

　D Total revenue will remain unchanged.

10 Price elasticity of demand

5 A price increase from $10 to $11.50 causes the demand for plant pots to fall from 1,000 units to 850 units per time period. What is the value of PED for the plant pots? *[1 mark]*

A −1.76

B −1.3

C −1.0

D −0.74

6 Suppose Casio sells 5,000 watches each month at a price of $100. Due to competition in the market, Casio reduces the price to $95. Subsequently, demand for its watches increases to 5,500 units per month.

a Calculate the PED for Casio watches. *[2 marks]*

b Explain whether it was a good decision for Casio to reduce its price. *[4 marks]*

7 The PED for rice in a particular country is known to be −0.4.

a Describe what would happen to the demand for rice if the market price increases by 5%. *[2 marks]*

b Explain **one** factor which affects the value of PED for rice. *[2 marks]*

8 Analyse, using an appropriate diagram, how an amusement park (theme park), such as Legoland, can use the concept of PED to decide whether or not to reduce its entrance ticket prices. *[6 marks]*

2 THE ALLOCATION OF RESOURCES

....

....

....

9 Teburu Desks sells 200 of its best-selling office desks per month at a price of $200 each. Following an increase in price to $230, the quantity demanded falls to 180 desks per month.

  a Calculate the PED for Teburu Desks' best-selling desks. *[2 marks]*

  ....

  ....

  b Explain, using your answer from Question 9a, how knowledge of PED can be of use to Teburu Desks. *[4 marks]*

  ....

  ....

  ....

  ....

10 Analyse the factors that determine the value of PED for educational textbooks. *[6 marks]*

  ....

  ....

  ....

  ....

  ....

11 Price elasticity of supply

1. What is the price elasticity of supply (PES) for a product that experiences a 5% increase in supply following a 10% price rise? *[1 mark]*

   A −2.0

   B −0.5

   C +0.5

   D +2.0

2. What is the PES for a product based on the information below? *[1 mark]*

Change in price	Change in supply
+8%	+2%

   A −6.0

   B +0.25

   C +4.0

   D +6.0

3. Which of the following is a use of PES? *[1 mark]*

   A to calculate changes in the general price level

   B to calculate consumer spending based on their disposable income

   C to estimate the changes in a firm's costs of production

   D to identify changes in the spending patterns of consumers

4. Which of the following is likely to have the highest value for PES? *[1 mark]*

   A haircuts at a local hair salon

   B organic oranges

   C original Picasso paintings

   D season tickets at Real Madrid Football Club

5. The market price of cherries falls from $5 per kilogram (kg) to $4 per kg, which causes the market supply to fall from 10,000 kg to 9,500 kg. What is the PES for cherries? *[1 mark]*

   A 0.05

   B 0.2

   C 0.25

   D 4.0

2 THE ALLOCATION OF RESOURCES

6 The PES for chocolate in a particular country is known to be +0.95.

   a Define 'price elasticity of supply' (PES). *[2 marks]*

   b Describe what would happen to the supply of chocolate if the market price increases by 10%. *[2 marks]*

   c Explain **one** factor which affects the PES for chocolate. *[2 marks]*

7 Suppose the market price of organic lemons increases from $4 per kilogram (kg) to $4.80 per kg, causing the quantity supplied to rise from 10,000 kg to 10,500 kg per month.

   a Calculate the PES for organic lemons. *[2 marks]*

   b Explain the results of your answer. *[4 marks]*

11 Price elasticity of supply

8 Explain, with reference to **two** different industries, the difference between **price inelastic supply** and **price elastic supply**. *[4 marks]*

....

....

....

....

9 Explain whether the PES for breakfast cereal is price elastic or price inelastic. *[4 marks]*

....

....

....

....

10 Analyse, with the use of appropriate examples, the factors that determine the value of PES for a product of your choice. *[6 marks]*

....

....

....

....

....

....

2 THE ALLOCATION OF RESOURCES

12 Market economic system

1 Which term describes the way in which an economy is organised and run? *[1 mark]*

   A barter system
   B economic system
   C market economic system
   D mixed economic system

2 Which of the following is **not** a disadvantage of the market economic system? *[1 mark]*

   A environmental concerns
   B incentives to work
   C income inequalities
   D social hardship

3 Which economic system relies on the market forces of demand and supply (in the private sector) to allocate resources? *[1 mark]*

   A barter system
   B market economic system
   C mixed economic system
   D production system

4 Which of the following is a disadvantage of operating a market economic system? *[1 mark]*

   A excessive bureaucracy
   B income and wealth inequalities
   C the lack of economic freedom
   D the lack of incentives to work

5 Which of the following is an example of wasteful competition in a market economic system? *[1 mark]*

   A decisions about how production should take place
   B environmental issues
   C excess packaging
   D social hardship

6 Explain, using a relevant example, how prices are determined in a market economic system. *[2 marks]*

....

....

7 Describe **two** features of a market economic system. *[4 marks]*

....

....

....

....

12 Market economic system

8 a Define 'public sector'. *[2 marks]*

b Analyse the costs and benefits of operating a market economic system. *[6 marks]*

9 Explain why there is greater inequality in income and wealth distribution in a market economic system than in a mixed economic system. *[4 marks]*

10 Discuss whether most people living in a market economic system (free market economy) benefit from such an economic system. *[8 marks]*

2 THE ALLOCATION OF RESOURCES

13 Market failure

1 Which of the following is **not** an example of market failure? [1 mark]

   A costs or benefits that affect third parties not involved in an economic transaction

   B goods that are over-consumed if left to the free market, such as tobacco and alcohol

   C private car parks in central business districts

   D public goods such as national defence and street lighting

2 Which of the following is an example of a merit good? [1 mark]

   A flood defence systems   C national defence

   B healthcare services   D street lighting

3 Which of the following is an example of a demerit good? [1 mark]

   A compulsory education   C public libraries

   B healthcare services   D sugary drinks

4 Which of the following is **not** an example of a demerit good? [1 mark]

   A alcoholic beverages

   B gambling services

   C junk food (fast food)

   D vaccinations

5 What is an example of an external cost associated with smoking? [1 mark]

   A health damage to people exposed to second-hand smoke

   B the cost of purchasing cigarettes

   C the pleasure smokers get from smoking

   D the production cost of tobacco

6 Give **two** examples of positive externalities of public parks. [2 marks]

....

....

13 Market failure

7 In 2018, South Africa introduced a 10% tax on sugary drinks, excluding fruit juices. This caused a subsequent increase in the average price of carbonated soft drinks. Explain **two** economic reasons for the introduction of a sugar tax. *[4 marks]*

....

....

....

....

8 a Define 'market failure'. *[2 marks]*

....

....

b Explain why governments provide merit goods. *[4 marks]*

....

....

....

....

9 The COVID-19 pandemic caused major disruption in labour markets across the world. The US Chamber of Commerce reported that more than 50 million workers quit their jobs in 2022, as many workers transitioned to other jobs in search of an improved work–life balance. In 2024, the European Commission also reported that labour and skills shortages are on the rise in all European Union member states, with almost two-thirds (63%) of small and medium-sized firms being unable to find the workers they need. Analyse the consequences of market failure caused by labour immobility. *[6 marks]*

....

....

....

....

....

....

2 THE ALLOCATION OF RESOURCES

10 In some countries, healthcare is funded for the majority of citizens by the government because of the perceived social benefits. Nevertheless, wealthier individuals often opt for higher-quality healthcare from private sector providers.

　a Define 'social benefits'. *[2 marks]*

　b Explain **two** advantages of charging people for private healthcare. *[4 marks]*

　c Discuss whether or not government funding of healthcare services will benefit society as a whole. *[8 marks]*

14 Mixed economic system

1 Which economic system uses a combination of both private and public sector output? [1 mark]

   A barter system
   B free market system
   C market economic system
   D mixed economic system

2 Which term describes the imposition of a price guarantee set above the market price to encourage supply of a certain good or service? [1 mark]

   A excess demand
   B excess supply
   C maximum price
   D minimum price

3 Which term refers to the government allocating resources in the economy? [1 mark]

   A competitive market
   B market economic system
   C private sector
   D public sector

4 Which of the following is a form of price control, involving the government setting the price below the market equilibrium in order to make products more affordable for consumers? [1 mark]

   A excess demand
   B excess supply
   C maximum price
   D minimum price

5 Which of the following can be provided by governments to encourage the consumption of certain goods and services? [1 mark]

   A minimum prices
   B minimum wages
   C subsidies
   D taxes

6 Explain, using a relevant example, the meaning of **privatisation**. [2 marks]

   ....

   ....

7 Explain the difference between **regulation** and **privatisation**. [4 marks]

   ....

   ....

   ....

   ....

2 THE ALLOCATION OF RESOURCES

8 a Explain what is meant by a **mixed economic system**. *[2 marks]*

....

....

b Analyse why most countries operate mixed economic systems. *[6 marks]*

....

....

....

....

....

....

9 Explain why there is less inequality in income and wealth distribution with government intervention than in a market economic system. *[4 marks]*

....

....

....

....

10 Explain, using an example, how quotas are a form of government intervention used to address market failures. *[4 marks]*

....

....

....

....

3 Microeconomic decision-makers

Student's Book Chapters 15–21

15 Money and banking

1 Which of the following is **not** a characteristic of money? [1 mark]

   A divisibility

   B durability

   C medium of exchange

   D uniformity

2 Which of the following best describes why durability is an important characteristic of money? [1 mark]

   A It allows money to be easily transported and used in transactions.

   B It ensures money can be easily divided into smaller units.

   C It ensures money can withstand physical wear and tear over time.

   D It guarantees that money will be universally accepted for trade and exchange.

3 Which of the following is **not** a function of a central bank or monetary authority? [1 mark]

   A controlling the money supply and interest rates to achieve macroeconomic goals

   B managing the country's foreign exchange and gold reserves

   C providing emergency funds to commercial banks and financial institutions that face short-term liquidity issues

   D providing loans and advances

4 Commercial banks lend more money than they receive in deposits, which increases the overall money supply in the economy. What is this process called? [1 mark]

   A advances

   B credit creation

   C foreign exchange

   D lender of last resort

5 Which function of money allows it to be used to settle debts that are to be paid in the future? [1 mark]

   A a standard of deferred payment

   B lender of last resort

   C store of value

   D unit of account

3 MICROECONOMIC DECISION-MAKERS

6 Distinguish between the roles of a **central bank** and **commercial banks**. *[4 marks]*

7 Explain **two** characteristics of money. *[4 marks]*

8 Explain **two** functions of money. *[4 marks]*

9 Analyse the roles of commercial banks. *[6 marks]*

10 In modern societies, individuals are increasingly using their smartphones to pay for goods and services using mobile platforms such as Apple Pay, Google Pay, PayPal, Alipay and WeChat Pay. Discuss the extent to which these online payment systems fulfil the essential functions and characteristics traditionally associated with money. *[8 marks]*

....

....

....

....

....

....

....

....

16 Households

1 What is the main source of income for most people? *[1 mark]*

A dividends

B interest

C profit

D wages and salaries

2 Which term describes income earned by an individual after income tax and other statutory charges have been deducted? *[1 mark]*

A disposable income

B gross income

C nominal income

D real income

3 Money intended for spending on goods and services within the next 12 months is known as *[1 mark]*

A capital

B capital expenditure

C current expenditure

D savings

3 MICROECONOMIC DECISION-MAKERS

4 Which of the following options is **least** likely to affect the level of savings and borrowing of households? *[1 mark]*

   A availability of credit

   B business confidence levels

   C household income

   D interest rates

5 Which of the following is the **least** likely determinant of the level of spending, saving and borrowing in an economy? *[1 mark]*

   A consumer confidence levels

   B inflation rates

   C interest rates

   D international trade policies

6 Define 'wealth'. *[2 marks]*

....

....

7 State **two** factors that determine the level of savings in an economy. *[2 marks]*

....

....

8 Explain **two** reasons why an individual might choose to borrow money. *[4 marks]*

....

....

....

....

9 Explain how the use of interest rates affects the amount of spending and savings in an economy. [4 marks]

....

....

....

....

10 Some countries impose high rates of income tax. Explain how direct taxes impact on the amount a person saves or spends. [4 marks]

....

....

....

....

17 Workers

1 Some professional footballers earn in excess of $1.5 million per week. What is the **most** likely reason for this? [1 mark]

   A Being a footballer is a seasonal job.

   B Some professional footballers have a unique set of skills and talent.

   C The job is high-risk so needs to be highly compensated.

   D The working life of a professional footballer is relatively short.

2 New law graduates in Country X can earn an annual salary of approximately $29,000 working in the public sector and $42,500 working in the private sector. Identify the **most** likely reason why a graduate may choose to work in the public sector rather than the private sector of an economy. [1 mark]

   A better promotion prospects and career progression

   B greater job security and pension

   C higher earning potential

   D more opportunities to earn bonuses

3 MICROECONOMIC DECISION-MAKERS

3 Following an increase in the national minimum wage (NMW), which of the following is **most** likely to reduce government expenditure on welfare payments? *[1 mark]*

A greater productivity of public sector workers

B increased consumer spending in the economy

C increased tax revenues from higher income taxes

D unemployed people may have a greater incentive to work

4 Women, on average, earn less than men. Which of the following is a possible economic reason for this? *[1 mark]*

A A larger number of women work part-time or have flexible working hours.

B More women are enrolled on medicine and law courses.

C More women are focused on their careers and delaying having children.

D There is a greater female participation rate in the workforce.

5 Which of the following is a disadvantage of specialisation of labour for a firm? *[1 mark]*

A The production process may become dependent upon a particular worker.

B The quality of the products increases.

C Workers become skilled in the job and more productive.

D Workers make fewer mistakes.

6 a Explain **two** non-wage factors that affect a person's choice of occupation. *[4 marks]*

....

....

....

....

17 Workers

b Use a national minimum wage (NMW) diagram to illustrate how this form of government intervention in labour markets can incentivise some people to join the workforce. *[4 marks]*

....

....

....

....

7 The UK government provides bursaries to people who wish to train to be teachers of mathematics, computer science and physics.

   a Explain **two** other ways a government may influence the supply of labour in an economy. *[4 marks]*

....

....

....

....

   b Explain how the UK government's intervention in the labour market for teachers of mathematics, computer science and physics can cause changes in the occupational mobility of labour. *[4 marks]*

....

....

....

....

3 MICROECONOMIC DECISION-MAKERS

8 Study the following table that shows the average earnings over a lifetime for all occupations in an economy. Explain the reasons why earnings typically change over a person's lifetime. (All figures are in US dollars.) *[4 marks]*

16 to 19 years	20 to 24 years	25 to 34 years	35 to 44 years	45 to 54 years	55 to 64 years	65 years and over
21,840	27,456	39,416	49,400	50,024	49,608	46,176

9 Koh Lanta is an island in southern Thailand and its main industries are fishing, farming and tourism. During the peak season, large numbers of workers are required to work in hotels, guesthouses, restaurants and other businesses related to the tourism trade. Analyse the factors that affect the demand and supply of labour in the tourism industry in Koh Lanta. *[6 marks]*

10 Frederica is an expert in producing hand-knitted garments. Analyse the advantages and disadvantages of specialisation of labour for an individual. *[6 marks]*

18 Firms

1 Which sector of the economy contains firms that provide services to the general public and other firms? *[1 mark]*

- **A** primary
- **B** public
- **C** secondary
- **D** tertiary

2 Which of the following is **not** a method used to measure the size of firms? *[1 mark]*

- **A** costs of production
- **B** market share
- **C** sales revenue
- **D** the number of employees

3 Which of the following is **not** an advantage of small firms? *[1 mark]*

- **A** easier to set up
- **B** greater degree of control
- **C** opportunities to gain economies of scale
- **D** quicker decision-making

4 Which type of growth occurs when firms expand using their own resources? *[1 mark]*

- **A** external
- **B** inorganic
- **C** mergers and acquisitions
- **D** organic

5 In the diagram below, what does the movement from point A to point B represent for a firm? *[1 mark]*

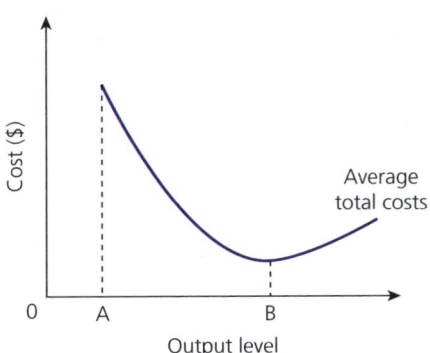

- **A** average total costs
- **B** diseconomies of scale
- **C** economies of scale
- **D** profit maximisation

3 MICROECONOMIC DECISION-MAKERS

6 Define 'diseconomies of scale'. *[2 marks]*

....

....

7 Give **two** examples of external economies of scale. *[2 marks]*

....

....

8 State **two** potential disadvantages of conglomerates. *[2 marks]*

....

....

9 Explain the difference between **backward** and **forward vertical mergers**. *[4 marks]*

....

....

....

....

10 Explain **two** disadvantages of (or challenges facing) small firms operating in the private sector. *[4 marks]*

....

....

....

....

19 Firms and production

1 What is the difference between **production** and **productivity**? [1 mark]

- **A** Production refers to the average output of goods and services, while productivity measures the efficiency of production.
- **B** Production refers to the total output of goods and services, while productivity measures the efficiency of production.
- **C** Productivity refers to the average output of goods and services, while production measures the efficiency of production.
- **D** Productivity refers to the total output of goods and services, while production measures the efficiency of production.

2 The production of which goods or services is **least** likely to be labour-intensive? [1 mark]

- **A** a Hollywood movie
- **B** a made-to-measure wedding dress
- **C** carbonated soft drinks
- **D** private piano lessons

3 Which economic term is used to describe or measure how well resources are used in the production process? [1 mark]

- **A** competitiveness
- **B** economies of scale
- **C** innovation
- **D** productivity

4 Which of the following options is **not** an effect of changes in investment on productivity? [1 mark]

- **A** higher output
- **B** improved efficiency
- **C** increased productivity
- **D** reducing the need for innovation

5 Which of the following advantages do **not** apply to capital-intensive production? [1 mark]

- **A** consistency in product quality
- **B** higher efficiency and output
- **C** job creation
- **D** lower long-term labour costs

3 MICROECONOMIC DECISION-MAKERS

6 a Define 'capital-intensive production'. *[2 marks]*

b Explain **two** reasons why a firm might choose to use labour-intensive production. *[4 marks]*

7 'The demand for factors of production (land, labour, capital and enterprise) is derived in demand.' Explain what this means. *[2 marks]*

8 Explain how productivity can improve due to an increase in investment expenditure in the economy. *[4 marks]*

9 Study the data below for two car sales firms over a typical month. The sales revenue for each firm is shown, as well as the number of cars sold and the number of sales staff involved.

Firm	Sales revenue ($)	Cars sold	Sales staff
Alpha Cars	284,850	15	5
Delta Cars	366,440	30	8

a Calculate the labour productivity as measured by the monthly sales per worker for both Alpha Cars and Delta Cars. *[2 marks]*

b Describe your findings. [2 marks]

....

....

c Explain why it might be difficult to determine whether Alpha Cars or Delta Cars is the more productive firm. [4 marks]

....

....

....

....

10 Explain, using relevant examples, why productivity is vital for the survival of firms. [4 marks]

....

....

....

....

20 Firms' costs, revenue and objectives

1 Which of the following is **least** likely to be a variable cost of production for a manufacturing firm? [1 mark]

A electricity charges

B overtime pay for workers

C rental payments

D wages for workers

3 MICROECONOMIC DECISION-MAKERS

2 Which term describes the costs of production that have to be paid regardless of how much a firm produces or sells? *[1 mark]*

   A average

   B fixed

   C total

   D variable

3 What is the correct label for the upward-sloping line shown in the graph below? *[1 mark]*

   A average costs

   B fixed costs

   C total costs

   D variable costs

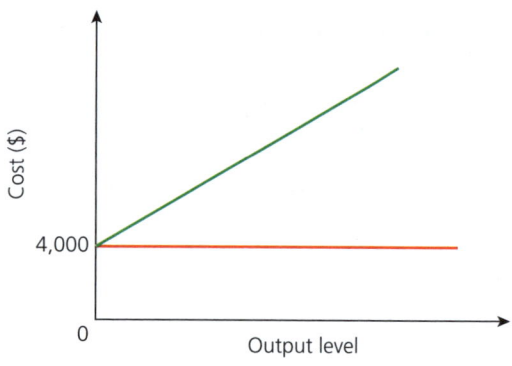

4 A firm's variable costs are $20,000 in a given week when its output is 2,000 units. Its fixed costs are $10,000. What is the value of the firm's average costs? *[1 mark]*

   A $5

   B $10

   C $15

   D $20

5 The payment received by a firm from the sale of its goods and/or services is known as *[1 mark]*

   A income

   B revenue

   C salaries

   D total costs

20 Firms' costs, revenue and objectives

6 Draw a fully labelled diagram to show both economies and diseconomies of scale for a producer. *[2 marks]*

7 The table below shows a firm's fixed and variable costs of production at different levels of output. Calculate the level of output where average costs are at their lowest. *[2 marks]*

Output (units)	Fixed costs ($)	Variable costs ($)	Total costs ($)	Average costs ($)
100	2,000	400		
200	2,000	760		
300	2,000	1,200		
400	2,000	2,320		

....

....

8 The table below shows the total costs of a firm at different levels of output. It sells each unit for $20.

Quantity produced (units)	20	30	40	50
Total costs ($)	200	285	360	460
Average costs ($)				

a Calculate the level of output required to minimise average costs. *[2 marks]*

....

....

b Calculate how many units the firm needs to produce and sell in order to maximise profits. *[2 marks]*

....

....

9 Study the data for a firm and answer the questions that follow.

Output (tonnes)	Total costs ($)	Total revenue ($)
0	1,000	0
100	2,000	1,500
200	2,800	3,000
300	3,600	4,500
400	5,200	6,000

3 MICROECONOMIC DECISION-MAKERS

a Calculate the unit price from the data in the table. *[2 marks]*

....

....

b Calculate the level of output at which average costs are minimised for the firm. *[2 marks]*

....

....

c Calculate the profit at each level of output. *[2 marks]*

Output (tonnes)	Total costs ($)	Total revenue ($)	Profit ($)
0	1,000	0	
100	2,000	1,500	
200	2,800	3,000	
300	3,600	4,500	
400	5,200	6,000	

....

....

10 Nina's Bakery has fixed costs of $8,000 each month. The firm's average variable costs are $3 per unit of output. The current level of demand at Nina's Bakery is 20,500 units per month. The average price of its products is $5.50.

a Calculate the monthly total costs of production at Nina's Bakery. *[2 marks]*

....

....

b Calculate the current cost per unit of output each month for Nina's Bakery. *[2 marks]*

....

....

c Calculate the profit if demand at Nina's Bakery increases to 25,000 units per month. *[2 marks]*

....

....

21 Types of markets

1 Which term refers to the various conditions which exist in different types of markets? [1 mark]

   A barriers to entry and exit

   B competitive markets

   C market structures

   D monopoly markets

2 Which characteristic applies to firms operating in competitive markets? [1 mark]

   A high barriers to entry

   B price setter

   C price taker

   D single supplier of a good or service

3 Which of the following is **not** a characteristic of highly competitive markets? [1 mark]

   A extremely low barriers to entry and exit

   B firms are price takers

   C low price elasticity of demand for a firm's products

   D the presence of many buyers and sellers

4 Which of the following is **not** a characteristic of monopoly markets? [1 mark]

   A economic efficiency

   B high barriers to entry and exit

   C price maker

   D the firm is the industry

5 Which of the following is **not** an example of a barrier to entry? [1 mark]

   A brand loyalty

   B economies of scale

   C high set-up costs

   D the number of firms in the industry

3 MICROECONOMIC DECISION-MAKERS

6 Explain the effect of having a high number of firms in a market on

   a price [2 marks]

   ....

   ....

   b profit. [2 marks]

   ....

   ....

7 Explain **two** advantages of a monopoly. [4 marks]

   ....

   ....

   ....

   ....

8 Analyse, using an appropriate demand-and-supply diagram, the impact of greater competition in the electric vehicles (EVs) market on equilibrium price and output. [6 marks]

   ....

   ....

   ....

   ....

   ....

   ....

21 Types of markets

9 Analyse, using relevant examples, the benefits of competition in a market. *[6 marks]*

....

....

....

....

....

....

10 Discuss whether or not monopolies are beneficial for consumers. *[8 marks]*

....

....

....

....

....

....

....

....

4 Government and the macroeconomy

Student's Book Chapters 22–28

22 Government macroeconomic intervention

1 Which term refers to an increase in a country's real gross domestic product (real GDP) over time? *[1 mark]*

- **A** economic growth
- **B** full employment
- **C** inflation
- **D** redistribution of income

2 Which of the following is calculated by using a weighted price index? *[1 mark]*

- **A** economic growth
- **B** full employment
- **C** inflation
- **D** redistribution of income

3 Which of the following is **most** likely to conflict with the government aim of high economic growth? *[1 mark]*

- **A** balance of payments deficit
- **B** employment opportunities
- **C** higher tax revenues
- **D** inflationary pressures

4 Which of the following is **least** likely to be a government aim in a free market economic system? *[1 mark]*

- **A** balance of payments stability
- **B** full employment
- **C** price stability
- **D** provision of welfare services

5 Which of the following is **not** used explicitly by a government to influence private sector producers? *[1 mark]*

- **A** investment
- **B** regulations
- **C** subsidies
- **D** taxes

6 Most governments strive to achieve full employment. Describe what is meant by **full employment**. *[2 marks]*

....

....

7 All countries aim to achieve economic growth by increasing real GDP. Describe what is meant by **real GDP**. *[2 marks]*

....

....

8 Explain why a government aims to redistribute income in the economy. [4 marks]

9 Explain why price stability is a key government aim. [4 marks]

10 In some countries, governments use subsidies to support farming in environmentally sustainable ways.

  a Define 'subsidy'. [2 marks]

  b Define 'environmental sustainability'. [2 marks]

  c Explain possible conflicts between economic growth and environmental sustainability as macroeconomic aims. [4 marks]

4 GOVERNMENT AND THE MACROECONOMY

23 Fiscal policy

1 Which term describes taxes paid from the income, wealth and profits of individuals and firms? *[1 mark]*

- **A** corporation tax
- **B** direct tax
- **C** income tax
- **D** indirect tax

2 If a government loosens fiscal policy in an attempt to expand the economy, what does this involve? *[1 mark]*

- **A** raising taxes and raising government expenditure
- **B** raising taxes and reducing government expenditure
- **C** reducing taxes and raising government expenditure
- **D** reducing taxes and reducing government expenditure

3 A government aims to expand total demand in the economy to boost national output and employment. Which policy should it use? *[1 mark]*

- **A** raise expenditure on education and healthcare
- **B** raise taxes and raise interest rates
- **C** reduce government spending and raise taxes
- **D** reduce taxes and reduce interest rates

4 Which statement does **not** outline how fiscal policy can be used to reduce unemployment in the economy? *[1 mark]*

- **A** A cut in taxes may increase consumer spending.
- **B** Government spending can create jobs in both the private and public sectors.
- **C** Greater government spending increases aggregate demand, causing the derived demand for labour to rise.
- **D** Lower interest rates increase the spending ability of households and encourage firms to invest more.

5 When does a budget surplus occur? *[1 mark]*

- **A** when a country exports more than it imports
- **B** when a country imports more than it exports
- **C** when government revenues exceed public expenditure
- **D** when public expenditure exceeds government revenues

23 Fiscal policy

6 a Define 'government budget'. [2 marks]

....

....

b Explain **two** reasons why a government might choose to increase public expenditure in the economy. [4 marks]

....

....

....

....

7 Some countries in the European Union, such as Sweden and Belgium, have high rates of direct taxes. Explain **two** reasons behind such a government decision. [4 marks]

....

....

....

....

8 In Country X the progressive tax rates are 12% (for those earning between $10,001 and $50,000 per year) and 17% (for those earning over $50,000 per year).

a Complete the table below and calculate the total amount of tax paid by an individual who earns $80,000 a year. [2 marks]

Income level ($)	Tax rate (%)	Amount of tax paid ($)
$10,000	0%	
$10,001–$50,000	12%	
$50,001+	17%	
Total tax:		

....

....

b Calculate the average rate of income tax paid by the individual. [2 marks]

....

....

4 GOVERNMENT AND THE MACROECONOMY

9 a Define 'fiscal policy'. [2 marks]

....

....

b Analyse how fiscal policy can impact on the supply side of an economy. [6 marks]

....

....

....

....

....

....

10 In some countries, income tax rates are deliberately set low. For example, the income tax rate is 10% in Andorra and Qatar. In contrast, higher taxes are often used by governments as a form of contractionary fiscal policy.

a Define 'contractionary fiscal policy'. [2 marks]

....

....

b Discuss whether raising income taxes is in the best interest of the economy. [8 marks]

....

....

....

....

....

....

....

24 Monetary policy

1. The amount of money in the economy at a particular point in time is known as [1 mark]

   A credit creation

   B monetary policy

   C notes and coins

   D the money supply

2. If a government loosens monetary policy in an attempt to expand the economy, what does this involve? [1 mark]

   A raising interest rates by reducing the money supply

   B raising taxes and raising government expenditure

   C reducing interest rates by increasing the money supply

   D reducing taxes and reducing government expenditure

3. Which of the following is **not** a monetary policy measure? [1 mark]

   A changes in foreign exchange rates

   B changes in interest rates

   C changes in money supply

   D changes in tax rates

4. Which of the following is a monetary measure that helps to reduce unemployment in the economy? [1 mark]

   A a cut in taxes

   B higher amount of government spending

   C investment in training and development

   D lower interest rates

5. An increase in interest rates, used to reduce overspending in the economy, is an example of [1 mark]

   A fiscal policy

   B loose monetary policy

   C supply-side policy

   D tight monetary policy

6. Define 'monetary policy'. [2 marks]

   ....

   ....

4 GOVERNMENT AND THE MACROECONOMY

7 Explain **one** reason why a government might choose to reduce interest rates in the economy. *[2 marks]*

8 Explain why a government might choose to use monetary policy. *[4 marks]*

9 Explain how monetary policy can impact the supply side of an economy. *[4 marks]*

10 Discuss the effectiveness of monetary policy in achieving sustainable economic growth. *[8 marks]*

25 Supply-side policy

1 The sale or transfer of public sector assets and industries to the private sector is known as *[1 mark]*

   A monetary policy

   B privatisation

   C public expenditure

   D supply-side policy

2 Which of the following is **not** a supply-side policy? *[1 mark]*

   A education and training

   B improving incentives to work

   C labour market reforms

   D reducing taxes and raising government expenditure

3 Which type of supply-side policy involves reducing or removing barriers to entry, in order to make markets more competitive? *[1 mark]*

   A deregulation   **C** lower direct taxes

   B education and training   **D** privatisation

4 Which type of supply-side policy involves changes to labour union legislation, welfare benefits and minimum wage laws in order to create better incentives to work? *[1 mark]*

   A deregulation   **C** labour market reforms

   B education and training   **D** lower direct taxes

5 Government policies designed to improve the quantity and quality (productivity) of resources in the economy by removing barriers to economic growth are known as *[1 mark]*

   A demand-side policies   **C** monetary policy

   B fiscal policy   **D** supply-side policies

6 Explain why a government might choose to use supply-side policies. *[4 marks]*

....

....

....

4 GOVERNMENT AND THE MACROECONOMY

7 Explain **two** supply-side policies a government could use if it wanted to improve the competitiveness of the economy. *[4 marks]*

....

....

....

....

8 Explain how a government can use supply-side policies to create incentives for firms to invest in the economy. *[4 marks]*

....

....

....

....

9 Explain, with the use of appropriate examples, why labour market reforms are a type of supply-side policy. *[4 marks]*

....

....

....

....

10 Discuss the effectiveness of supply-side policies in achieving an economy's macroeconomic objectives. *[8 marks]*

....

....

....

....

....

....

26 Economic growth

1 Which term refers to an increase in the output of an economy and its productive capacity? [1 mark]

   A economic boom

   B economic growth

   C economic recession

   D economic recovery

2 Which of the following is **least** likely to be a reason to aim for economic growth? [1 mark]

   A to create employment opportunities

   B to raise standards of living

   C to raise tax revenues

   D to tackle the problems associated with poverty and inequalities

3 Which term refers to the total spending on goods and services by individuals and households in an economy over a given period of time? [1 mark]

   A consumption expenditure
   C investment expenditure

   B government spending
   D net export expenditure

4 Which term refers to the value of national income adjusted for inflation to reflect the true value of goods and services produced in a given year? [1 mark]

   A nominal economic growth
   C real economic growth

   B nominal gross domestic product
   D real gross domestic product

5 Which of the following is a consequence of an economic recession? [1 mark]

   A higher interest rates
   C lower levels of government expenditure

   B higher levels of unemployment
   D lower levels of household debt

6 Explain **two** causes of economic growth. [4 marks]

....

....

....

....

4 GOVERNMENT AND THE MACROECONOMY

7 Use the data in the table to calculate the gross domestic product (GDP) per capita (to two decimal places) in Mauritius and New Zealand. *[2 marks]*

	Mauritius	New Zealand
GDP (USD billion)	14.4	253
Population (million)	1.26	5.31

Source: Mauritius and New Zealand GDP per capita, September 2024, World Bank, Trading Economics website

....

....

8 a Define 'recession'. *[2 marks]*

....

....

b Explain **two** causes of a recession. *[4 marks]*

....

....

....

....

9 The diagram below shows a typical business cycle. Identify appropriate labels to complete the diagram. *[3 marks]*

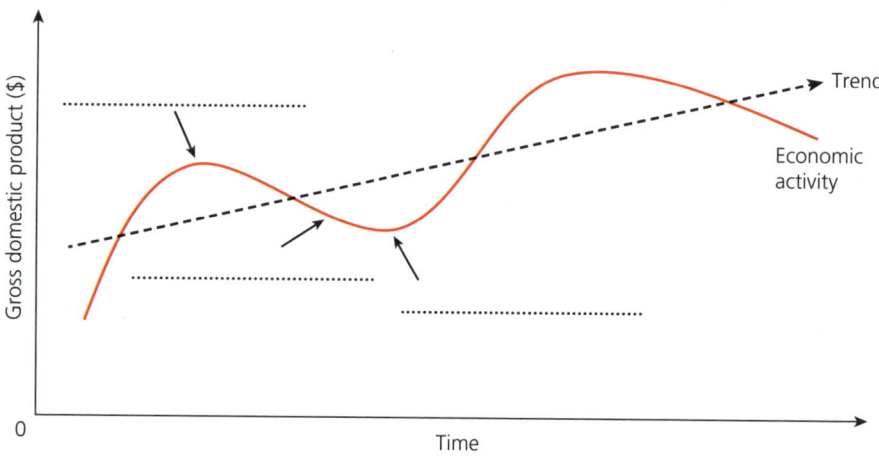

10 Discuss whether an increase in government spending will lead to economic growth. [8 marks]

....

....

....

....

....

....

....

....

27 Employment and unemployment

1 What is the name given to the situation when people of working age are both willing and able to work but cannot find employment? [1 mark]

- **A** classical unemployment
- **B** unemployment
- **C** unemployment rate
- **D** voluntary unemployment

2 Which type of government policy is best suited to deal with imperfections in the labour market? [1 mark]

- **A** fiscal policies
- **B** monetary policies
- **C** protectionist policies
- **D** supply-side policies

3 Which of the following is generally regarded as the most severe form of unemployment? [1 mark]

- **A** cyclical unemployment
- **B** real wage unemployment
- **C** structural unemployment
- **D** voluntary unemployment

4 GOVERNMENT AND THE MACROECONOMY

4 The table below gives population data for a particular country which has an official retirement age of 65. *[1 mark]*

Total population	66 million
Aged 0–14	17 million
Aged 15–64	38 million
Aged over 65	11 million

If the unemployment rate is 7%, the number of unemployed people is

A 2.66 million

B 4.62 million

C 10 million

D 28 million

5 What is the main cause of frictional unemployment? *[1 mark]*

A changes in demand for certain goods and services

B people changing jobs

C people choosing not to work

D wages set higher than the market equilibrium

6 Explain what is meant by the **unemployment rate**. *[2 marks]*

....

....

7 Calculate the unemployment rate in a country that has a population of 46.6 million people, of which 30 million are employed and 2.7 million are unemployed. *[2 marks]*

....

....

8 Explain which type of unemployment is most associated with a downturn in the business cycle. *[2 marks]*

....

....

9 Explain how the International Labour Organization (ILO) measures unemployment. *[2 marks]*

....

....

10 Explain **two** economic advantages of a fall in unemployment. *[4 marks]*

....

....

....

....

28 Inflation

1 Which of the following will tend to cause an increase in a country's rate of inflation? *[1 mark]*

   A discount food prices at the major supermarkets

   B lower consumer and business confidence in the economy

   C lower rates of interest

   D subsidised energy prices

2 Which statement suggests why savers lose out during times of inflation? *[1 mark]*

   A Money loses its ability to act as a store of value.

   B Money loses its ability to act as a unit of account.

   C Real interest rates become negative during inflationary periods.

   D Real interest rates become positive during inflationary periods.

3 If the weighting for food in a country's Consumer Price Index (CPI) exceeds that for shoes, what does this indicate? *[1 mark]*

   A Food is considered to be more important to the average household than shoes.

   B On average, the price of food has increased more than the price of shoes.

   C The average household buys more food than shoes.

   D The average household buys more shoes than food.

4 GOVERNMENT AND THE MACROECONOMY

4 If the CPI in a country rises from 115.2 to 116.8 in the subsequent year, what is the inflation rate? *[1 mark]*

- **A** 1.39%
- **B** 1.6%
- **C** 1.68%
- **D** 16.8%

5 The table below shows CPI data for Country X. Based on this data, in what year were prices at their lowest? *[1 mark]*

Year	CPI	Year	CPI
1	102.2	3	103.9
2	104.6	4	105.4

- **A** Year 1
- **B** Year 2
- **C** Year 3
- **D** Year 4

6 Calculate the rate of inflation if the CPI drops from 135.6 to 130.2. *[2 marks]*

....

....

7 A basket of goods and services currently costs $1,500. Calculate how much it would cost if the CPI fell from 125.5 to 121.1. *[2 marks]*

....

....

8 Explain the difference between **demand-pull** and **cost-push inflation**. *[4 marks]*

....

....

....

....

9 a Define 'inflation'. *[2 marks]*

....

....

b Define 'deflation'. *[2 marks]*

....

....

10 Study the data for Country X below and answer the questions that follow.

Item	Consumer Price Index	Weight
Clothing	120	15
Food	130	30
Housing	140	40
Other	125	15

a Define 'Consumer Price Index' (CPI). *[2 marks]*

....

....

b 'The typical household in Country X spends more money on food than on clothing.' Explain this statement. *[2 marks]*

....

....

c Complete the table below and calculate the weighted CPI in Country X. *[2 marks]*

Item	Consumer Price Index	Weight	Weighted CPI
Clothing	120	15	
Food	130	30	
Housing	140	40	
Other	125	15	
Weighted CPI			

....

....

5 Economic development

Student's Book Chapters 29–32

29 Living standards

1 Which factor is **not** included in the calculation of the Human Development Index (HDI?) *[1 mark]*

   A Consumer Price Index (CPI)

   B gross domestic product (GDP) per head

   C life expectancy at birth

   D mean years of schooling and expected years of schooling

2 Which of the following is a limitation of using real GDP per head as a measure of the standard of living in a country? *[1 mark]*

   A It does not account for inflation over time.

   B It does not consider income earned in every industry.

   C It does not consider the size of the population.

   D It does not reflect the distribution of income and wealth.

3 Which term refers to the total value of all goods and services produced within an economy, adjusted for inflation and divided by the total population? *[1 mark]*

   A CPI

   B HDI

   C income distribution

   D real GDP per head

4 From the limited data below, which country is most likely to have the highest standard of living? *[1 mark]*

Country	GDP ($ billion)	Population (million)
A	129.7	18.5
B	153.6	150.0
C	43.2	15.2
D	89.9	9.2

   A Country A

   B Country B

   C Country C

   D Country D

5 Which of the following is **not** a limitation of the Human Development Index (HDI), specifically, to classifying countries in terms of their living standards? [1 mark]

   A Inequalities in income and wealth are ignored.

   B Longevity, education and income are not the only factors that affect human development.

   C The components of the HDI are indiscriminately weighted equally.

   D The definitions of economic development and standards of living are subjective.

6 Explain **two** reasons for differences in income distribution within countries. [4 marks]

....

....

....

....

7 Damascus in Syria is rated by the Economist Intelligence Unit as one of the least liveable cities in the world. Explain **two** reasons why this might be the case. [4 marks]

....

....

....

....

8 Explain **two** reasons why an increase in real GDP per capita may not result in a rise in living standards in a country. [4 marks]

....

....

....

....

5 ECONOMIC DEVELOPMENT

9 Economic growth is associated with an improvement in living standards.

    a Describe what is meant by **living standards**. *[2 marks]*

    b Analyse **two** ways that a government can improve the living standards in its country. *[6 marks]*

    c Discuss whether or not economic growth in a country always results in higher living standards for its people. *[8 marks]*

10 Discuss which of the two countries below is most likely to have lower living standards based on the economic development indicators given in the table. *[8 marks]*

Country	GDP per capita ($)	Life expectancy (years)	Expected years of schooling	Mean years of schooling
Guinea	508	59	8.8	2.6
Sierra Leone	496	51	9.3	3.3

Source: World Bank (GDP per capita), UNDP (other data)

....

....

....

....

....

....

....

30 Poverty

1 Which of the following is **least** likely to be an indicator of poverty in an economy? *[1 mark]*

A homelessness and inadequate housing

B hunger and malnutrition

C inadequate income

D unemployment

5 ECONOMIC DEVELOPMENT

2 What exists when there is extreme outright poverty in an economy, i.e. average income is equal to or less than $2.15 per day? *[1 mark]*

  A absolute poverty

  B poverty line

  C poverty trap

  D relative poverty

3 What is experienced by those who have a lower standard of living in comparison to the average member of society? *[1 mark]*

  A absolute poverty

  B poverty line

  C poverty trap

  D relative poverty

4 Which of the following is **not** a United Nations Sustainable Development Goal (SDG)? *[1 mark]*

  A clean water and sanitation

  B reduce, reuse, recycle

  C reduced inequality

  D zero hunger

5 Which of the following is **least** likely to be a cause of poverty? *[1 mark]*

  A high public debt

  B high rates of tax

  C low GDP per capita

  D low literacy rates

6 Explain **two** reasons why absolute poverty is a concern for any government. *[4 marks]*

....

....

....

30 Poverty

7 Explain **two** reasons why improved education can be an effective policy to alleviate poverty and redistribute income in an economy. [4 marks]

....

....

....

....

8 According to the World Bank, the GDP per capita in Mozambique was $608.4 in 2023 (about $1.67 per day). Explain why poverty is a concern for the government in Mozambique. [4 marks]

....

....

....

....

9 Explain any **two** causes of poverty. [4 marks]

....

....

....

....

10 Apart from improved education, explain any **two** policies that can be used to alleviate poverty. [4 marks]

....

....

....

....

5 ECONOMIC DEVELOPMENT

31 Population

1 Which factor is **most** likely to raise the average age of a population? *[1 mark]*

- **A** a higher birth rate
- **B** a higher death rate
- **C** improved health technologies
- **D** net migration

2 Which factor is likely to increase the population in a country? *[1 mark]*

- **A** greater female participation in the workforce
- **B** higher cost of living
- **C** higher fertility rates
- **D** increased education expenditure

3 The net migration rate is calculated by the formula *[1 mark]*

- **A** birth rate − death rate
- **B** death rate − birth rate
- **C** number of emigrants − number of immigrants
- **D** number of immigrants − number of emigrants

4 Which statement about population distribution is correct? *[1 mark]*

- **A** Low-income countries generally have a lower average age than high-income countries.
- **B** Most countries are experiencing ageing populations.
- **C** Poorer countries tend to have lower dependency ratios.
- **D** The gender split is uneven in most countries, with more females being born.

5 The median age of the UK population was 35.4 years in 1985 and is projected to be 42.2 years by the year 2035. What does this suggest about the population in the UK? *[1 mark]*

- **A** It has a declining birth rate.
- **B** It has a declining death rate.
- **C** It has a positive population growth rate.
- **D** It has an ageing population.

6 a Define 'death rate'. *[2 marks]*

....

....

b Define 'birth rate'. *[2 marks]*

....

....

31 Population

7 Explain **two** factors that affect the rate of population growth. *[4 marks]*

....

....

....

....

8 Explain the difference between **underpopulation** and **overpopulation**. *[4 marks]*

....

....

....

....

9 The chart below illustrates the growth in Mexico's population between 2013 and 2023.

Mexico's population, 2013–2023

Source: Mexico population summary (source: Consejo Nacional de Población), Trading Economics website

  a Explain what has happened to Mexico's population in the time period shown. *[2 marks]*

....

....

5 ECONOMIC DEVELOPMENT

b Explain **two** economic problems which could be associated with the continual rise in the size of Mexico's population. *[4 marks]*

....

....

....

....

c Discuss whether or not the population growth will bring about negative consequences for the Mexican government and the natural environment. *[8 marks]*

....

....

....

....

....

....

....

....

10 In 2024, the population of Japan had an average age of 49.4 years. In the same year, the average age in Indonesia was only 30.1 years. The fertility rate was 1.2 in Japan and 2.1 in Indonesia.

a Describe what is meant by an **ageing population**. *[2 marks]*

....

....

b Describe what is meant by an **optimum population**. *[2 marks]*

....

....

c Analyse the impact of the high median age and low fertility rate on Japan's population structure. [6 marks]

....

....

....

....

....

....

d Analyse the impact of the low median age on Indonesia's dependency ratio. [6 marks]

....

....

....

....

....

....

32 Differences in economic development between countries

1 Which term refers to an increase in the economic well-being and standard of living within a country? [1 mark]

    A economic development

    B economic growth

    C gross domestic product

    D production possibility curve

5 ECONOMIC DEVELOPMENT

2 Which factor does **not** account for differences in the economic development of countries? [1 mark]

    A exchange rate fluctuations

    B investment in education and healthcare

    C population growth

    D productivity levels

3 Which of the following is **least** likely to be an indicator of economic development? [1 mark]

    A gender equality

    B greater self-esteem

    C higher interest rates

    D political freedom

4 Which sector of the economy do most people in less economically developed countries tend to work in? [1 mark]

    A primary

    B public

    C secondary

    D tertiary

5 Attracting foreign direct investment (FDI) will enable a country to enjoy higher levels of [1 mark]

    A imports

    B productivity

    C savings

    D unemployment

6 Define 'natural resources'. [2 marks]

....

....

32 Differences in economic development between countries

7 Explain, with reference to investment in the economy, the importance of savings. [2 marks]

....

....

8 Explain how differences in population growth between countries have an impact on their level of economic development. [4 marks]

....

....

....

....

9 As an economy develops, there tends to be a shift away from reliance on primary and secondary sector production. Explain why this is the case. [4 marks]

....

....

....

....

10 Analyse how healthcare and education have a direct impact on a country's economic development. [6 marks]

....

....

....

....

....

6 International trade and globalisation

Student's Book Chapters 33–36

33 Specialisation and free trade

1 Which of the following is **most** likely to result from greater international specialisation? *[1 mark]*

 A Consumers have more choice of goods and services.

 B Employees benefit from greater job satisfaction.

 C Employees benefit from greater variety in the nature of their work.

 D Households benefit from lower prices.

2 International trade that takes place without any form of protection (barriers to international trade) is called *[1 mark]*

 A dumping

 B exchange

 C free trade

 D international relations

3 Which of the following is **not** a benefit of free international trade and exchange? *[1 mark]*

 A choice

 B economies of scale

 C efficiency gains

 D transportation costs

4 Which of the following is a disadvantage of international specialisation? *[1 mark]*

 A changes in efficiency

 B changes in productivity

 C changes in international competitiveness

 D changes in labour turnover

5 Which outcome does **not** apply to free trade? *[1 mark]*

 A access to a wider variety of goods and services

 B economic growth

 C increased efficiency and specialisation

 D retaliation from trading partner countries

33 Specialisation and free trade

6 Explain, with the use of relevant examples, what is meant by **trade barriers**. [4 marks]

....

....

....

....

7 Explain, with the use of examples, how division of labour is a form of international specialisation. [4 marks]

....

....

....

....

8 Explain **two** reasons why specialisation can lead to higher incomes for workers. [4 marks]

....

....

....

....

9 Analyse why overspecialisation can be problematic for the economy. [6 marks]

....

....

....

....

....

6 INTERNATIONAL TRADE AND GLOBALISATION

10 Discuss, with the use of examples, the advantages and disadvantages of international specialisation for firms. *[8 marks]*

....

....

....

....

....

....

....

....

34 Globalisation and trade restrictions

1 Which of the following is an objective of trade protection? *[1 mark]*

- **A** to create domestic jobs
- **B** to improve the economic efficiency of domestic industries
- **C** to increase the demand for domestically produced goods and services
- **D** to reduce the costs of international trade

2 Which method of trade protection is used to directly reduce the price of exports? *[1 mark]*

- **A** embargoes
- **B** quotas
- **C** subsidies
- **D** tariffs

3 What is the name given to the act of selling exports at artificially low prices, below those charged by domestic firms, and often at less than the cost of production? *[1 mark]*

- **A** administrative barriers
- **B** dumping
- **C** embargoes
- **D** subsidies

34 Globalisation and trade restrictions

4 Which term describes the increasing interconnectedness and interdependence of the world's economies, cultures and populations? [1 mark]

   A exchange

   B globalisation

   C international trade

   D protectionism

5 Which of the following is **not** a cause of globalisation? [1 mark]

   A an increase in the level of global trade

   B customers across the world having similar purchasing habits

   C increasing numbers of migrant workers across the world

   D increasing use of trade protection methods

6 Define 'trade protection'. [2 marks]

   ....

   ....

7 Explain **two** possible economic reasons why consumers in the USA might import fewer cars from the European Union. [4 marks]

   ....

   ....

   ....

   ....

8 Explain **two** causes of changes in globalisation. [4 marks]

   ....

   ....

   ....

   ....

6 INTERNATIONAL TRADE AND GLOBALISATION

9 Explain the effects of globalisation on

   a the environment [2 marks]

   ....

   ....

   b income distribution. [2 marks]

   ....

   ....

10 Discuss whether the government of a country should protect domestic industries from foreign competition. [8 marks]

....

....

....

....

....

....

....

....

35 Foreign exchange rates

1 Which of the following is **least** likely to be a reason for buying and selling foreign currencies? [1 mark]

   A government intervention in currency markets

   B higher prices of goods and services

   C migrant workers' remittances

   D speculation in foreign exchange markets

2 In a floating exchange rate system, what determines an equilibrium foreign exchange rate? [1 mark]

   A commercial banks operating in the private sector

   B demand and supply of currencies in the foreign exchange market

   C speculators in the foreign exchange market

   D the central bank or central monetary authority

3 Who are the individuals or firms that buy and sell foreign currencies with the aim of making financial gains? [1 mark]

   A central banks

   B commercial banks

   C monetary authorities

   D speculators

4 In which exchange rate system is the exchange rate determined by the market forces of demand for and supply of the currency? [1 mark]

   A fixed

   B floating

   C managed

   D mixed

5 Identify, with reference to the diagram below, the option that does **not** explain the change in the exchange rate of the New Zealand dollar. [1 mark]

   A an increase in interest rates in New Zealand

   B greater demand from British households for New Zealand exports

   C more British tourists visiting New Zealand

   D more firms from New Zealand investing in Britain

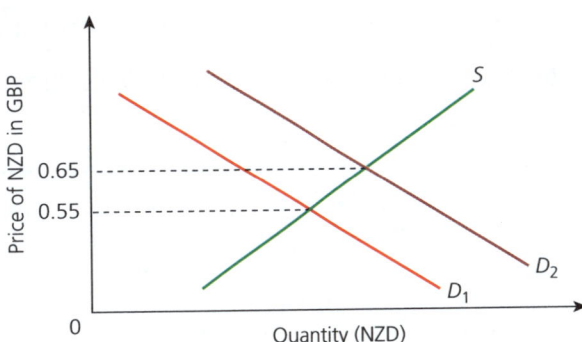

6 INTERNATIONAL TRADE AND GLOBALISATION

6 Define 'exchange rate'. *[2 marks]*

....

....

7 Suppose the exchange rate between the US dollar (USD) and the euro (EUR) is USD1 = EUR0.73. Calculate the price for customers in Europe of buying textbooks priced at USD70 from the USA. *[2 marks]*

....

....

8 Suppose the exchange rate between the British pound (GBP) and the Hong Kong dollar (HKD) is GBP1 = HKD10.5. Calculate (to two decimal places) how much it costs a British tourist (in pounds) to buy an iPad in Hong Kong that is priced at HKD6,000. *[2 marks]*

....

....

9 Suppose that the exchange rate between the Australian dollar (AUD) and the British pound (GBP) is AUD1 = GBP0.57, while the exchange rate between the Australian dollar and the Hong Kong dollar (HKD) is AUD1 = HKD6. Calculate the exchange rate of the British pound against the Hong Kong dollar (to two decimal places). *[2 marks]*

....

....

10 Although the Chinese government controls the value of its exchange rate, it has been known to allow the yuan (the Chinese currency) to appreciate.

   a Explain what is meant by an **appreciation** in the value of a currency. *[2 marks]*

....

....

   b Analyse the likely effects of China's currency appreciation on its exports and imports. *[6 marks]*

....

....

....

36 Current account of the balance of payments

1 What is the name of the record of a country's exports and imports of physical goods? [1 mark]

   A the balance of payments

   B the current account

   C the invisible trade balance

   D the visible trade balance

2 Which of the following is **not** part of a country's net income flows and transfers? [1 mark]

   A bank deposits held in overseas banks

   B interest, profits and dividends

   C money sent home from people working abroad

   D money spent on intangible products

3 What is the correct formula for calculating a country's current account on the balance of payments? [1 mark]

   A trade balance + net exports

   B visible balance + invisible balance

   C visible trade balance + invisible trade balance + net income flows and transfers

   D visible trade balance + invisible trade balance − net income flows and transfers

4 What is a result of a sustained current account deficit for the domestic economy? [1 mark]

   A higher exchange rate

   B higher standards of living

   C higher total demand

   D higher unemployment

5 Which policy is **least** likely to result in an improvement in the current account of a country? [1 mark]

   A lower exchange rate

   B lower income taxes

   C subsidies for export-driven firms

   D trade protection policies

6 INTERNATIONAL TRADE AND GLOBALISATION

6 Describe, using the data below, what has happened to Country X's balance of trade. *[2 marks]*

Year	Invisible balance ($bn)	Visible balance ($bn)
1	15.2	12.3
2	16.7	13.4

....

....

7 State any **two** components included in the current account of the balance of payments. *[2 marks]*

....

....

8 Explain how it is possible for a country to have a deficit on its visible trade balance (trade in goods) but still have a current account surplus on its balance of payments. *[2 marks]*

....

....

9 Study the data below and answer the questions that follow.

Trade balance for Country D ($billion)	
Exports	103
Goods	87
Services	
Imports	113
Goods	87
Services	
Visible balance	
Invisible balance	10
Trade balance	

a Define 'visible balance'. *[2 marks]*

....

....

b Calculate the missing figures in the data above for Country D. *[4 marks]*

....

....

....

....

10 Analyse how a fall in the exchange rate can reduce a country's current account deficit on its balance of payments. *[6 marks]*

....

....

....

....

....

....

Reinforce learning and deepen understanding of the key concepts covered in the latest Cambridge IGCSE™, IGCSE (9-1) and O Level Economics syllabuses (0455/0987/2281) with this updated Workbook. An ideal course companion or homework book for use throughout the course.

» Develop and strengthen skills and knowledge with a wealth of additional exercises that perfectly supplement the updated Third Edition Student's Book.

» Build confidence with extra practice for each lesson to ensure that a topic is thoroughly understood before moving on.

» Consolidate knowledge and skills with updated exercises based on authentic and up-to-date contexts and problems.

» Keep track of students' work with ready-to-go write-in exercises.

» Save time with all answers available FREE to download from: hachettelearning.com/answers-and-extras

This text has not been through the endorsement process for the Cambridge Pathway.

Also available:
Cambridge IGCSE and O Level Economics Student's Book, Third Edition 9781036010737

The Student's Book is endorsed for the Cambridge Pathway.

For over 30 years we have been trusted by Cambridge schools around the world to provide quality support for teaching and learning.
For this reason we are an Endorsement Partner of Cambridge International Education and publish endorsed materials for their syllabuses.

 Visit us at hachettelearning.com

ISBN 978-1-0360-1075-1